Hoshang Merchant (b. 1947) has been writing poetry exclusively in English since 1965. His first poem was published in America in 1973 by the MLA, Utah. He did his apprenticeship at the university in America and on the road in Greece, the Middle East and India. He finally published in 1989 when he had a desk at the University of Hyderabad with Writers Workshop. These poems cover twenty years of his publications in magazines, chiefly *Kavya Bharati*. He is an Indian poet deeply rooted in his family traditions while at the same time expressing the glory and pain of being a pioneering poet in gay India.

Sufiana
p o e m s

HOSHANG MERCHANT

HarperCollins *Publishers* India

First published in India in 2013 by
HarperCollins *Publishers* India

Copyright © Hoshang Merchant 2013

ISBN: 978-93-5029-639-4

2 4 6 8 10 9 7 5 3 1

Hoshang Merchant asserts the moral right to be identified as
the author of this work.

All the poems in this collection first appeared in *Kavya Bharati*,
issues 2–23, 1990–2011.

HarperCollins *Publishers*
A-53, Sector 57, Noida, Uttar Pradesh 201301, India
77-85 Fulham Palace Road, London W6 8JB, United Kingdom
Hazelton Lanes, 55 Avenue Road, Suite 2900, Toronto, Ontario M5R 3L2
and 1995 Markham Road, Scarborough, Ontario M1B 5M8, Canada
25 Ryde Road, Pymble, Sydney, NSW 2073, Australia
31 View Road, Glenfield, Auckland 10, New Zealand
10 East 53rd Street, New York NY 10022, USA

Typeset in 12/15 Crimson Regular at
SÜRYA

Printed and bound at
Thomson Press (India) Ltd

Contents

Sufiana

Prologue: Return to My Native Land

I was the sea-driven one
Who landing built a sun-temple
Laughed at a cunt-king's milk-teeth
Went about my sunset marriage
Casting my dead skyward

I was the one who on plantations
Secretly kept wives
And sat on the village council
I harnessed water-power
Sailed a raft to China
Struck iron ore, a million from old bottles
I worshipped Victoria

Who tasted my fruit
And knighted me
I invested my dark children with sudrehs
Took ever whiter wives
Who danced, drank, played canasta
The Chinese made their frocks and dice
Some followed Blavatsky, saw spirits

I was busy building the great peninsular railway
Some killed tigers, whence the adage:
Killing tigers in my pyjamas
(Whence Groucho took it).
Some took to transmigration, some to banking
Buying up pieces of rock from Aden to Zanzibar
A 100,000 laboured on my cotton

('Einstein was a German Zarthoshti')
Some kept men marching on their stomachs
Some kept mad princes in pence
Some devoted to Iran, fallen women or boys:
Even in dire straits bowlers
Our scandals covert, our law British
One plotted against Parliament

No more Parsees at Oxford
No more British citizenship
No more clubs and cocktails
No more plantations:
Given to Gandhi when our cocoa kids
Joined the torching labour
No more

Failing to gain guarantees
We changed to homespun
Saluted the rising sun—
Liberated women ran off with niggers
The conscience-stricken went into slums
The conscienceless married into wealth
Money more money readymoney

Our comedy never ended:
She waits each 4 for her busdriver lover
He beats her up each 10 of the clock
She delivers each September
Twelve to a team
—All fashioned in a patois our own.
Where was the Word?

Given me the Avesta
Purged by fire
By Alexander conquering
Conquered by Arab—
Till the land, father sons, kill an enemy
Thus spake Zarathushtra
Our masters and slaves took revenge linguistically

I played for stocks in their tongue
Loved Pola Negri and Chaplin
Screamed nightmares and poems
Signed birth, marriage, death certificates
Divorce papers and suits in their tongue!
Most loquacious of animals, I, the Parsee, was
Tongueless

I covered up:
Tooled around in sedans
Dozed post-dhansak at the Ripon
Ordered in servantese
Loudly intoned an Avesta unknown to god or beast
By sea, river, fire; even Mary's shrine
Valiantly transplanted Zal and Zohak to Gujarat

Why conquer the world when a drop abolishes it?
Our daughter-in-law, a new Indian empress
With our son made the bomb:
Wipe out thy neighbour—
What defoliation couldn't, sterilization took
So it became that we, a master-race
Were victims of the whip we held

Ever the lord and ever the jew:
What is your memory, your dream and nightmare?
What hour of the day can you cherish?
Who'll reimburse your slave; snatch your wealth?
Who decolonize your heart?
What land can you claim
You who don't even have graveyards?—To New Haven?
You sons of wanderer-gentlemen whose sons wander again

Finale:
Droning priests descend a well
Where birds perch
The body/a naked stone
Its soul shivers on a hair-thin bridge
(In Heaven philanthropies don't wash:
It perpetuates poverty)
Intoning—

I am the sea-driven one
Who landing built a sun-temple
Laughed at a cunt-king's milk-teeth
Then cow-hoof on head
Went about my sunset marriage
Casting my dead skyward

The River of the Golden Swimmer
To Whabiz, Darling Sister (1946–2011)

> '*The road led into the mountains, where a great gorge brought us to the river of the Golden Swimmer. He was a shepherd, a Leander, who used to swim across to visit his beloved, until at last she built the truly magnificent bridge by which she also crossed. At length we came out on the Azerbaijan highlands, a dun sweeping country like Spain in winter. We passed through Miana, which is famous for a bug that bites only strangers, and spent the night in a lonely caravanserai where a wolf was tethered in the courtyard. At Tabriz the police asked us for five photographs each (they did not get them) . . .*'

—Robert Byron, *The Road to Oxiana*, 1937

1

Last month
On the last day
At midnight
My sister died:
A neat end to a neat life
When a childhood playmate goes
The whole world goes

But the leaves are full of children . . .

2

A poem is not a puzzle to be solved
But an experience to be lived through

My sister, my spouse . . .

3

The soul trembles
        on a hair-thin bridge
                for the fearful
But for the righteous
        It becomes a broad highway

4

In Tabriz
The Golden Swimmer swam nightly
                to his beloved
She built him a bridge to lessen his troubles
And she too would cross over, often . . .

5

My sister gave me the key
        to how to love without a body
        I simply unlocked the mystery

6

Now I go shopping with other sisters
              Brothers phone for recipes
So while sister-soul goes shopping
Brothers are miraculously fed on earth

(For Usha Mudiganti, Delhi)

Light
In Memoriam: A.K. Ramanujan (d. 13 July 1993)

'When elated think of darkness
When depressed think of light'
—Buddhist precept

1

I think of light
in my darkened room
this morning at seven

2

The house of light!
Light flooded it from the valley
We could barely see
The house floated on the afternoon
We kept our bearings
Seeing this way
And that way at sea.

3

'The beauty of her two eyes
slayeth me
Its power none may sustayne.'

4

Beauty too is light. And birth:
Some dark room opens a crack
A beam of light dances out
It whirls in space awhile
Then is put out
Our going is a blowing out; as of a lamp

5

This morning
My head
My bed
Float out
on a sea of light.
The body is bound
The spirit travels like Jesus on the waves.

Sharjah College, UAE
27 July 1993

Birth of Poetry

And so it came to pass
in my young age
when I had no name
that I came to belong to a race
—the race of poets

The jewel box of the radio
lit in the night
with names of magic stations:
Remember Montevideo?
—A mountain shone forth
wholly itself; yet an emblem, all mountain

And so poetry was born
As Professor Aguiar droned on
On the AIR about John Wain
and the Bomb
Mother and we sat up all night
to hear Marian Anderson
The voice that comes once in a 100 years
—that night it had come into our fractious Bombay home

Poetry is the voice
that first makes women out of virgins
and then out of women makes widows
Their men dead of toil or of bullets
And so a million Madonnas
rising out of the sea
as a million Mount Marys
sink back into the sea with their blessings

Men are angels with clapboard wings
And the more they flap them
                              the less they fly
But the poetry is that they try
so every lazy poet sleeping late every day
pisses on all the world's workers
And anyone mocking a single martyr
spits on all the world's young idealists

So that when the poppies peep out
of the rocks amid the Iranian grain
Then suddenly it's the Monet print gone bitterly
                                              haywire
And instead of a parasol you see a descent
                                      of parachutes
And a heavenward ascent on a prayer
                    Heaven's gold key round a 16-year-old neck
                    a bomb belt round the waist

What waste
if Ifti had been killed
reciting that poem against the Pak dictator
Now he has more sense
And wouldn't do it again
      Since he has survived
He's always carried a body menu
      the paraphernalia of poets and prostitutes

O nude boy!
Between your breasts grows the grain of Lebanon
Below your navel curl the grapes of Lebanon
And Narcissus tears through the streets
      on a Ford Bronco
Or rides to Tucson, a young Moses
      glimpsing a promised land

I saw the moon tonight over Chicago's towers
A second-day moon when sisters wish for brothers
My sister has taken up a pen/she does not weep
She sits beside me at the movies/pitying to see me
      weep and weep
Over the fate of celluloid poets   Reeling
Over not blood but ink

And Shahid Ali returns each summer
to Kashmir in search of a poem:
a 14-year-old Orpheus runs into the ground
                    springing back yearly as a narcissus
And Anais saying all workers and poets will be killed by
                    power
Or, O for a lover who doesn't snore!

Where did Anais' legacy end up?
—With a young lumberjack
an Orpheus out of the West
Heir to her blood-rhythms; jazz-rhythms
To the Prairie School
and of Duchamp playing champ with buddy
over Beatrice Wood

Ah, Beatrice again!
Dante's and D'Annunzio's and Duchamp's
and our own Beatrice of our very alley
Ifti telling me at the pride parade:
Dante sd/- if you don't stand up and be counted
                    when the time comes
                    there's hell to pay
—A slight misquote, perhaps
                    amid the drag queens' swishing trains

And the Hyderabad sisters, thoroughbreds
                              Chicago-reared
reading my poem before the Michigan ocean
Having nothing for comparison
                    but Gibran's *Prophet*
And I saying: Yes, yes
I, a poet with no capital
                    except the jam between his toes
The bird that eats will fly away
What bird? What food? What flight!
Tell Monu and Donna, spoilt Midwest intellects
                    they owe all poets their living
                    butterfly, butterfly!
                    Mariposa, farfalla!

Just as I, then a mere kid
owed a living to Purdue's Felix Stefanile, B.A.,
who taught me Neruda
And to Bruce Woodruff who put Dresden's bombers in
    his Inferno
And now my Indian girl-student
follows me up Felix's Sparrow Street
saying: You taught me Donne
        And that's my debt to you
So with every new Ananda
                    I must but be a new Buddha

Why were you making eyes at me, Walt Whitman
                              from the tomatoes?
Shahid, what witness does your voice bear
                              to the prairie wind!
Ifti, why did you go mad in your Lakeshore cage aux
   folles
                              on the fortieth floor
What does elevator ascension have to do with poetry?
                              Go down, down

Lie down in darkness

Do you have alligators in India?
              asked the prairie boy at the Greyhound
—No, but crocodiles bite just as good
The whale that languishes in the Aquarium
                    The porpoise that weeps
And I weep at the Auditorium
My sister listens in the dark
         I weep because she is dying
And the wind that moans through the wheat
         Mows down her garden leaves
The prairie stars shine now over my bed
(I gathered up my long hair in sheaves
              the better to write this)

And my sister sleeps
And I hear heartbeats of babies
     we did not birth
But to be born after my sister and this poem
                are gone

And so it came to pass
in my young age
when I had no name
that I came to belong to a race
—the race of poets.

            Memorial Day Weekend, Chicago
                    1995

Reading Arabic Poetry the Day Iraq Fell

For I am a stranger
Beloved Iraq
Far distant, and I here in my longing
For it, for her . . . I cry out: Iraq

And for all the orange groves
And all the olive groves
And the beds of rice topped with chicken
And beds of pearls in the seabelly
And in the oyster belly the pearl
But in the belly of the earth: oil

A new Mongol has come
And we have to stoke our tandoors
                    with our children's bones
And we have blood on our plates
Blood in our beds
But, our invaders have our blood on their hands

For I am a stranger, Iraq
I'm not of your blood
And the lady of Hyderabad
In her starched white cotton saree
                    Adorned with kalamkari

Speaking pure Dakhni
Guarding her precious Arabic books from theft
Under the shadow of the mosque dome copied from Tunis
  said:
This is the pearl that came to us from Tunis
But it is just an old mosque now
I read all the poets of Baghdad
And even the passport thieves fell silent
Because poetry is a passport in itself

And it is also a transport
I wept pure tears

Crystalline like pearls
Which cleansed all infections
Then why does the Mongol only understand blood
                    Oil and blood
                    Blood and oil
The seabeds of Bahrain are polluted by oil

There are no pearls of the purest water now
The purest water now is tears
The eyes of desert martyrs do not turn pearls
                    They remain hollow
Mosque minarets now are factory chimneys
                    And I smell burning human flesh
Adonis   Adonis will not rise from the Euphrates
                          this spring

Water is pure cyanide
And people prefer to drink saltwater
    Refine it and drink it
    Like their own tears
Men have died before machines
    raining death from the air
For a lost notion of knighthood
    It is indeed now night We're all benighted
When will they crucify the returning Christ, Iraq!
When will they bathe in the blood of the new Buraq?

An Indian Poem for Baghdad

And now her trees are slowly drinking water
                      after the summer drought
And her two eyes shine like two moons on the water
The waters of my native city that stretch to Arabia
And beyond: And there in the desert Baghdad awaits rain

The rain of mercy over Baghdad, god's gift
Or has god abandoned Baghdad?

I can hear the trees slowly drinking water in her gardens
Her two eyes shine like moons over the waters
But my lover, 27 years old, lies under the mountain
In his grave, eating mud and drinking rain

I want to sleep under the earth with my lover
I'd very much like to sleep under the earth
And be with you Baghdad in an unnamed grave
Because when you pray for one dead loved one
                      you pray for all the dead

Terry Taimur Murtuza Mirza, the guitar player of
   Hyderabad
A Picasso among cooks and decorators
Says it's always good to think of death
It is a sign of the rain of god's mercy
Because the people of this earth have forgotten mercy:

Ali Abbas, 12 years old, was protected by a mother's embrace
When it rained bombs instead of mercy from the skies
A mother between the sky and death
                              protecting a 12-year-old
She died for him but he lost both his arms
The arms that hugged a mother

What rain will wash this blood?
How many monsoons will it take?
The house and the garden are gone
After all we are all tenants on this earth
As we water the earth with our tears and blood
And the dying father left his palm-prints on the wall

The wall is all that remains
And the palm-prints
But his entire family is gone
And the next rain will wash away his last signs too
His last signs imprinted upon our hearts
And the heirs of Haroun al-Raschid beg in the streets of
    Baghdad

Our hearts are gardens we grow
For another's use
And now the garden is weed-choked
And no rains come
For in ancient India and Sumeria god too was dry clay

Made into a statue
Invested with godhead
Raining mercy for centuries
But the marauding mobs in their dry land
Have turned these gods to clay again
And no rains come . . .

Who has the key?
The thief has the key to the museum-god
Sold in 12 pieces in the modern market
We know the price of oil
                    but not the value of history

At the morgue lies the bride
Killed by a jealous husband
For war starts not in the skies
But like rain in the marriage bed
And a husband lies in the same graveyard erect
First burnt by fire, then strangled by jealousy's torment

Whose earth is it anyway?
The earth is his who can make it rain
The tears of mercy from two eyes
That shine like my mother's in my nursery
Through her hopes and fears:

And now the rain comes
I can hear it rain in Bombay
Nourishing the roots in my mother's garden
And now her palms
                              wear the new crowns of leaves . . .

Vaikunt

Every 16 years
The doors of Heaven open
To let in the good
If they die a day later
They have to wait 16 years
Yudhisthira waited
For his dog to follow him to Heaven
The hero would not forget a friend even in death
Be wise live and learn
Teach and delve
So when you go
Your good deeds go with you
Like good children's prayers
Like Yudhisthira's dog

(For Sujit Mukherjee)

Iran

Memory comes
as wave upon wave
of fire
Washes over me
Burns into my skin
Burnishes the paper I write on
The flagstones I tread on
In alley after alley after alley
Looking for the nursery
Where heroes birth and die
Birth and die
Cradle to grave
(The grave a cradle)
Where mothers come mourning
Laying sprigs of gladioli
Spring bulbs that bloom again
from the loam mixed with blood
Here he sowed the dragon teeth
Here 10,000 heroes sprouted
Here they rode off on horseback
Here they were felled, bare backs
to the wind and the rain
Sprouting as ears of grain
For this they were made
                    and prepared

As the sacrifice.
On each nation's gate it is written:
        Let the grain die
Ground into bread
Eaten in graveyards in death
as at a picnic in life
And the river washes the stones
And the domes watch over the river
As it rushes to the sea
Waves and waves of emotion
Wash over me
I look for my lover
In chai-khaneh and Zurkhaneh
He's not there, not there
He's here with me
Laughing from the grass

Eulogy for Virgil Lokke,* My Teacher

Virgil sits
reading Physics
at table
Four days short of death
Virgil doesn't care
for cosmic dances
He's concerned with physical detail:
Weight, matter, density, gravity
Virgil knows
When you go/you just go

It is winter in the valley
Virgil is short of two weeks
and a month for his 83rd year
There aren't any more *Eclogues* to be written
The leaves have turned with the year
      And are buried
The snakey gravel path he constructed
         à la the philosophers
Leads nowhere
It only goes from here to there
Snaking all the way

*Virgil Lokke taught at Purdue University and was known for his
scepticism.

Virgil, where is Dante?
Didn't you design the city-church's steeple?
Did you not hurl yourself upon the deeps
                          from up there?
Take me with you, Virgil
For there is no comfort here
All is false
The demons are of our own making
And hell is not elsewhere

Did not the leaves turn red for you
                          last autumn?
Did not the glow-worm dispel dark
                    in the glen
                    on your last night?
You went into the night

You just had your soup
Your dessert was here/not elsewhere
It is all here/'There' being not there

Did Vivaldi strain again in church
At your funeral as he did at your wedding?

The Fourth season:
Is there a fifth?
I hear one straining in my breast
Ravi Shankar on the sitar
This India morn
And I feel re-born, a lover
You Virgil, would have liked
                    the mathematics of it:

Two boys one young
                    one old
Stand on the river's brink
And hear the enchafed flood
It is the tide of blood rushing in
And then the earth grows cold

                    Green me, beloved teacher
                    I too turn cold with the leaves.

New Year Poems, 2001

1

I await the coming of the new year
As I await the coming of a lover
Who has been away a month
but it seems a year

2

I have been here
Half a hundred years
And before me my father
And before him, his
But the future is my lover

3

One thousand years have touched
The sleep of the boy I was
Who slept before the sea
Under a mirror

Even now in my sleep
Lightning strikes the glass
And my mother, lamp in hand
Goes around the house
As if searching for something in the dark
                        Then the rain on the dry tiles

4

Lightning strikes
and plays on the edges of the sky
As light around the edges of a photograph
Whose heart is dark

Why did not the lightning gently pass
That fateful night a 1,000 years ago
When Christ was crucified

At least the wind is kind
It blew his name to the four corners of the globe
Yet earthworms are blind

5

I leave the door open
for the year like my lover to enter

Sometimes he is the honoured guest
And sometimes my heart is dark
I cannot find the spark
to re-ignite an unfinished conversation

6

The world is my body
His body
My body upon his body
The world's body

7

The look we exchange sometimes
is the look the lamb exchanges
with the butcher who sharpens the knife

Lightning!
Lightly pass over my house tonight
Do spare this world its extinction, another year

8

And a boy dies in Kashmir
An innocent lamb
whose blood dyed the grass

9

A man and a woman walk to the end of night
A man, a woman and a friend walk to the end of night
They are the star, the treetop, the sky
Freedom is always for the one who thinks differently
Freedom is only for the one who thinks differently
We were all to be free
But we feel the pull of the chain
                    We hear the cry

Bombay, 12 March 1993

This is an attempt
to write an epic
It is not Homer
It is Hell

1

Where were you
when the bombs went off?
At the stock exchange
The airlines office
Where were you
when they burnt the docks?
Sitting pretty at Wayside Inn
having cheesecake!

2

The man in the image
had aged imperceptibly
He had become his father
So nothing had changed
Where were you?

3

The Parsee, Miss India
shot to fame in Star Trek
Now bald no more
Onto her third husband in Toronto
—Who cares?

4

Remember the burning taxi at Bombay
The Burning Giraffe of Dali's
The broken perfumerie:
'Original almond oil guaranteed!'
The queen quoting *Pakeezah* movie queens
when Bombay Mahim was burning:
The perfect parody of living by one's
                              heartbeats!

5

Dad, blind and squinting
into the 8.15 news on TV
What would they do to his black money?
And you squinting into his windowpane
Son no more: But a visitor
to an aquarium seeing blind fish
                   swim by

6

Between City Hotel and Centaur Airport
They shot an arrow
into the void
The Otter club caught it
The Sea-Rock club caught it
At Hare Krishna you at a non-karmic meal

7

Where were you
when all was burning?
Where was the small flame to warm
When the big flame burnt?

8

The house is empty
The children are desolate
The curtains are torn down
Your smoke still clings to them
The tea cup is lonely
Your kiss still lingers on it
The smoke of your cigarettes
                mingles with the bombs
rising to seventh heaven:
Where are you?

9

Hindu claims you
Moslem claims you
She was mine he says
She was mine say the others
You were once and only once mine

10

In ancient India
a woman once superbly married
five brothers
Another tried to rape her
She stands for raped womanhood
But the Brahmins aetherealized her
Saying she's the human soul
bound to the five senses

11

If man has five senses
Why is he so senseless?

12

They had come in '47
to Baramullah Kashmir
Raped the sisters
singing Ave Maria
I had once met
The Hero of Gilgit
—an innocuous Sherpa

They could not bring back
        an inch of lost soil
They could not regain a single lost tree
But they came all the way to Bombay
        to kill a beautiful deer

13

She was the beautiful deer
Zenobia of Palmyra
Her feet didn't touch earth
I, her love, had taught her flight
Her bangles jingled as she laughed
She sailed across the street
        like a tall ship at sea

She was billowing with pride
She was the dower of a king overseas
She was port and chancel
She was Arab and Jew
She was her own value
and worth her weight in gold
She could not be bought
She would not be sold
—So they killed her

14

Whoever did this dastardly deed
Is not fit to be called human
The city is not on its knees
The city is on its feet

My poem is its own testimony:
A thing has value because it exists.

Homage to Derek Walcott

'We do not have a Homer singing the sea
And we do not even have a Walcott' (sd/- KNC)
—And I cannot be Homer
But I could've been Walcott for

I lived on the sea   But
Our civilization is riverine
And if we reach the sea we are One
                    that is to say None
that's philosophy not poetry

We have 1000s of miles of sea
But no poetry of the sea
Unless we count *Chemmeen*
And before it the port of Poompuhar

We look inwards
The Greeks outwards
The Arabs too: outwards and onwards
And the Egyptian Cleopatra

between man and man
that is to say between sea and sea:
each of her men being an emperor
And she a woman, riverine

And I was Cleopatra
dancing down the street
A butterfly balanced on my nose
Going to who knew what conquests?!

And the Arabs
taking the Malabar boys
Making them into men
And taking their women

Making them Moslem
And the Mappila was born
And the tree of the coconut
was Kalpavriksha

Fruit and seed
Thatch and root
Coir and rope
Kernel and boat

The men set out to sea
They had their songs
The women stayed home
They had their tears

Vasco da Gama came
And before him the Arab to Sind
And after him the English by sea
to Chennai and Chandannagore

Imagine the Christian
Sweating blood in the marshes
Imaging the convert
Sweating blood on the Cross!

There was no rain
There was no rice
Then there was Christ
And then there was grain

And the sea gave fish
And the land gave loaves
And god gave English
And we were all British

Seamen going to sea
Seamen going to war
Man-of-war going down
to the bottom of the sea

These were pearls which were
                his eyes

bones became coral
bodies became water
And the world was an empire
On which the sun never set

The sea is deep
The sea is cruel

The sea is ebb and tide
The sea sings repetition

The sea joins lands
The sea divides lands
As sex joins and divides
Man and woman

The sea is contradiction
The sea is reconciliation
The sea is deep
The sea is cruel

What O sea do you bring us?
—I bring you pearls and coral and Death
Where O sea do you take us?
—I take you on a sea change

So the Malayalee speaks Arabic
And the Sinhalese speaks Malayalam
So rubber grows in Kerala
And tea sprouts in Irien Java

And everything is changed
Into something rich and strange
So yellow marries black
Imagine their babies

I found one fettered
to a sugar cane stalk in Hawaii
That was her history
She'd rechristened herself 'Ai', a poet

Sounds like a scream of pain?
You bet—the Christian God gives you grain
And Arab marries Somali
Imagine their babies

I found one tied
to his grandfather's magic carpet
On which he transported his Swahili slaves
Back to Oman

He flew Air Oman
And dreamt Swedish women
Of course he's called Mohammed
And by now he'd be dead of AIDS

But Islam saved him
Or alternating fasts
With fornication saved him
Saved, for what?

Cleopatra was tied to a chariot
And ridden through Rome
That was her triumph
Christ was tied to a tree, Ixion to a wheel.

That was theirs
We were tied to the English tongue
We untied our various sacred threads
Threw them into a well or a sea

(Everything sacred goes to water
Everything profane goes to earth)
The language we took to
Made us spring wings

We took to air
And Caliban curses no more
in his own tongue
But in an alien tongue now his own

O sea wash our sins away
O water purge us of our bestiality
O Ganges going to a sea
Drown us not but resurrect us

Into our own individuality
(Ah! The sin of sins!)
Is there ever a top dog
                    among dogs?

Caliban was a cannibal
He ate his own race
What do you name one
Who eats other races?

When I eat grain
He becomes my god
Then god becomes my blood
Then grain becomes my flesh

Nightly my lover
eats me in bed
Daily the sea
Grinds my bones to stone

My ancestors prayed to Ava—
Goddess of the sea
O Goddess protect us from perfidy
O Lady submerge not Bombay City

And my poor father
And his poorer grandfather
All prayed to the lady of the sea
And now stepmother steps in her mules

Into a family tradition
She isn't fitted for
For Mother Mary came out the sea
And before her Venus

And after them the Black Mary
Crossed the sea
Selling herself on board
Christ accepted her in the Holy Land

My mother dreamt Mary
When she lost her first baby
And Mary promised her many
When she tried to drown herself in the sea

We all drown at birth
Choked on our own sails
We all hope to resurrect at marriage
But really we only resurrect at death

My lovers say I'm looking for a poem
My students say I'm looking for god
But I'm neither looking for lover nor poem nor god
But for Death which is all of these

Death is the sea
Rajiv went to Lanka
and dealt death
so they came here by sea

To kill him.
Rama went to Lanka
to *seek* Sita
The bear and the monkey helped

to set Sita free
And the squirrel's pebble for the bridge
earned her a stroke
—the stripes on her back

Rajavarmana went to Kamboj
built Angkor
A Ship of Death
Be ready to die, the Buddha said

And the fire heard him
And slaked its thirst
And the water in the pot
Cooled its heat

The parrot saw a forest fire
And brought the sea in his beak
And the sparrow was saved from the eagle
With the barter of Buddha's own body

For stories are also a sea
And all the stories sink
to the bottom of the sea
I was Caliban

Now I aspire
To be Prospero
I write in blood and semen
                    And I break my pen.

                              (For K. Narayana Chandran)

An Arizona of the Mind

1

An unseen land
is more real
because it's Imaged: Imagined

There's a myth about a man
going to hell for a woman
Hell's lord let her go
But he looked back
          and lost her
Yet she returns each spring

2

At the zenith
of Prescott Pass
where scrub gave way to juniper
The White Mountain was glimpsed
Not stone   but mist

3

Sister wanted to spend the night tired
in a ghost town, Jerome
The vast hotel/The abandoned goldmine
And men still panning gold
Fixing old Oldsmobiles and Vauxhalls
(Things don't rust here)
At a bend in the road
Transfixed, marooned
the hill hotel overlooking the valley
—a boat before a sea
What sinuous rills, ascents, staircases!
Mirrors throwing back light
Or taking you in
From them look out laughing gold-diggers
And sad, lonely eyes of '20s' men

4

The Canyon's southern rim
All red stone
And suddenly Sedona
like the mystery of the Oriental Sun temple:
Stone idol and supplicant
Carved by wind and winding river
Action of water on stone
Everything washes away/Only water survives

And the boy in the bowl
of the parking lot
His hair rippling like light
His laughter, rippling like light
What dream had he seen last night?
How did the Navajos interpret it?
Had he decided to be a moon-child
A bird-child transformed on a mountain
Double-sexed like an arrow-weed?

I saw the eagle circle over us thrice
I will remember that sight

What a man dreams in his heart
is his real self/It is his wish

5

Then sister took ill
on the mountaintop   Breathlessness
And I promised Whabiz   blood-transfusions
                              transplants
Mine:
She was after all mine
(And we only momentarily forget we're all dying)
But she being small could only fit
                      a child's heart

Cursed once again by man-curse
Once again I wished   to mother
                          to child
The roads on the map, all arteries
                all choice

6

Then it rained
I remembered India's rains
But the leaves are narrower here
And the rain comes down noiselessly
Good dreams come from the moon
                   The bad, from the sun
Sun and moon brother and sister
Chase each other
So the two are always on the run
Indian mothers teach children
                  to hoard their dreams

And a rainbow appeared

7

How we cheered as children
at the *Living Desert* matinee
The Disney cat on the saguaro tree
with the coyote baying beneath!

8

In the beginning was fire
And then when lava congealed
Mountains painted green and red appeared

When the rock cooled the land was fissured
From this fissure I rescue my poem

Majnun in the desert and Ghalib's cry:
Seeing the Sahara my home I remembered
Lifting stone, Majnun   His head he remembered

9

Nogales (N.M.) last night on TV
Children of the sewers
connecting desert and desert
Living like rats or bats
who respect no borders

Telling the newsmen:
If you're ever homeless you're welcome here

10

The sudden crack of a pistol-shot!
It's John Wayne shooting a movie
in Greer: the oldest inn in Arizona, 1860
And *he*'d left no tips

Next morning's help found $5 bills under every cover

And Jane Wyman suddenly smiles
from the mirror
turns and is gone

11

Don't shoot here
You'll kill deer

Three looming fates we came upon
on the highway   Earth coloured
Stood a moment dreaming
the dream of time

Startled and were gone
in the direction they came from

Only the mother went the other way
                    to rescue her fawn

12

And when Marco Polo
was already in China
The Indians still chiselled on the rock here
Labyrinths from the loom of time

13

Then cowboy took to cowboy:
Don't make love
You'll frighten the horses!

14

And in cowboy suit
after church Dodge Phelps' CEO
Helps his peroxide lady out of a Ford Bronco
Shimmering mirages out
                    for Sunday lunch at the only inn
                    in a one-horse town
Real myths having ridden on . . .
He flattened Copper Canyon into the ground
Dante's hell too was such a bottomless pit

15

I knock on a door
Someone answers Who's here (Hoosier?)

I'm a homesteader 100 years late
Come to a New Harmony, West
The Temple in ruins eternal
And a train departs who knows to what Belsen
I correspond with Carthage and Rome
                              They reply
Delhi, CA lies a highway away

Where in what Temple will I find
Again   That old American mind?

Virgil and Xenobia   Anais and Carmela
I owed them a life I lost

16

At sunset
flying over Ispahan
from a fogged plane window
like an old man
tracing the contours of a youthful love
I see the camel-humped mountain
But not one blue dome
All Alexander's army trapped in the desert

Mutinying to go home

On the world's other edge Marco Polo's Gobi
On this the old artist-lover's cry
                    Bihzad! Bihzad!

Come home!

Epilogue:

And now it rains in Swat
The desert taxi driver can see it in my eyes
                    in his rearview mirror
Yet nothing comes of loss but loss
I shut my eyes and see
New cosmogonies
Scenes never seen
but suspiciously like old ones
Aren't all oceans the nascent waters of our birth?

I will be the cat that climbs the cactus tree
And I am the coyote baying at me

It rains the rivers of India in my eyes
And from the cracked mirror my mother the poem smiles.

(For Agha Shahid Ali)
June 1995

Konya

A pilgrimage was promised me
                    by my horoscope
I dreamt of Borobudur but came to Konya
A pilgrimage is supposed to change you

1

So from Istanbul the bus veered steeply down
Past the thickly wooded Black Sea coast
Away from Trabezon's towers to the south

2

Already there was death on the way
As in the Mongols' day:
The way was sleeted over
And somebody lay dead

3

Who was it that lay dead?
The tourist pimps lay in wait
But a kindly cabman delivered me to my door

4

Next morning I went in search of Rumi
I already knew the shape of his tomb
And someone on the way pointed out the street
                                        where he danced mad

5

First I visited his Master Shams
                                        and then I visited the student
My student had called me
I had come

6

And Master and student lay side by side in death
As they must've lain in life
But they were both teachers
                        And their graves were topped by their hats

7

And their rival Chelebi who was jealous
                        of the Master's other favourites
Also found a place in the capacious graveyard

8

For if someone was jealous in Love's court
Rumi courted him a few days
And moved on

9

The tintinnabulation of the goldsmiths
                    had driven him mad
The small hammer on the tympanum
                    had driven him mad

10

And the dance he danced
Led him to the circles of the spheres
Like the stars reflected in the planetarium pool
                    Led to the stars in the real sky

11

Friend lies here with friend
Lover lies here with lover
Not to lie here is a lie

12

And at night they close Rumi's museum
(for this is what they call his mosque since Ataturk)
And a Sufi in green praying at the door
Bought a poor vendor's entire store of tomatoes
So he would not sleep hungry
(And he wasn't even a Turk, he was American)

13

Everyone in the town knew
How F-16s bombed Iraq and Afghanistan
And how Rumi had converted one American heart

14

First one then ten and then ten million
Got converted on the dusty way to Konya

15

I never dreamt of coming to Konya
But ever since I came I hear the goldsmith's
                    tintinnabulation in my ear
I too dance with the celestial spheres.

Dharamsala Canto

And so it came to pass again
That when I had a modest name
as a poet and teacher
the man who gave me my name
and my body, my father
died
And I came back to the Dalai Lama
after 21 years   for blessings

The Dalai hadn't aged
though he was 60
There are those whose karma
makes them lose their homeland
But they gain the world:
The Dalai and I were one . . .

It was a long way to Lhasa
The Dalai had dispensed with even a bow
A brisk 'Tashi Delek', Hello!
With a firm Texan-style handshake
had replaced the prostrations
21 years ago we two had shaken hands
I, alone among a sea of Tibetan refugees

And my old teacher Ngawang Dhargey
who'd asked me pointedly to forget him
Had gone on
to become a living Buddha in New Zealand
Dead, blinded by diabetes
after a long life of goodness
He would have turned in his urn
to become thus deified in death!
And I had much anger and lust in me yet
But you do not get very far with anger
                              or lust

Now the Dharma teacher
Played himself in a film
Compassion without money doesn't go far
And talked of dolphins' mercy rescuing sailors
The Buddha as Turtle offering his vitals
                        to the ants
Feed! So you may live and I may die

And Ben Vine of London
gives me the first smile
in a class full of bad karma people
They're because they made the Bomb:
Die! So I may live
And they now wash off karma
                        with a little dharma

And Ben Vine remembers
Our Lord Jesus Christ from a Tuscany childhood
The evil in the Tuscan church frescoes was cosmic
Ben squinted to see the devils fly
                or plunge down to hell

O! What a Sunday sermon!
But Christ and the Buddha
         are always compassionate
And in Mexico the children still call
Christ 'The Rain God', all wet with tears

And I remember the Chinese Hell Tortures
from Bombay's Prince of Wales Museum:
Little porcelain dolls
burning, beating, tonsuring
gouging out eyes
tongue-piercing with pincers, red hot
I winced: I will be good out of fear
Out of fear and not out of guilt

Because Adam ate the apple
                  Not I
Because Cain killed Abel
                  Not I
I am not guilty
But I AM responsible for my action

And the Chinese say the Lamas
Beat, tortured, raped the Tibetan peasant
No, says Sonam, translator
                          from Santiniketan
Han Suyin lies
She is Beijing's stooge!

I am in a hell of anger and lust:
All men are androgynes
And all androgynes are Bodhisattvas
Mercy, mercy, mercy, mercy, mercy.

I wrap up the world in my napkin
                          over coffee and cake
The world has visited Tibet:
American breakfast like Mom used to make
Grandma's apple-pie/Best pizza east of Italy . . .
All for a price, of course
But you couldn't go wrong
on your way to the dharma . . .

And you do not go very far with gluttony
Gluttony, anger and lust:
I dream I feed my body to the birds—
Here Vulture! Eat my flesh!
And I dream I love a young man
                          in Orissa
The snow eagle circles the Triund peaks
                          White

And a boy blanks out in a daze
                    of whiteness
In the Tibetan opera boys are birds
                    girls, fillies

Among all the coffee
          and all the talk
The illiterate Tibetan boy-waiter
          offers me a chair:
'Do not squat on the cold ground
                    with hippies
You are a teacher, you deserve a chair',
his simple silent gesture seems to say
I appreciate it enough to note it here

The hoopoe sits on a thorn bush
The crow on the rhododendron
The eagle on the snow peak
The clouds gather
The mists come
And the rain/Sometime the mist is mountains
          Sometime the mountain, mist
The hippies scatter
to gather in Leh
It has snowed in Manali
It has rained in Delhi
          (Hottest summer in 54 years
          Earliest rains in 97 summers)

A 1,000 have died in Orissa in the heat
And I remember my boy

Burning in heat
Cooled by the dharma . . .
The Gaddi shepherd brings out his family
                              along with the bullocks
To till the family plot
There is shame in ferrying foreigners
          200 metres for Rs 20 in a rickshaw
But that built them these stone walls
And saved them from the slavery
of following sheep up slopes
And smelling all winter in rained-upon
                              wool

And Krishna cowers
under Radha's saree
in a Kangra rain
Life of the immortals in miniature example:
If you have to, lift Goverdhan mountain
So all living creatures can shelter under you
In the rain and the storm

Nothing has really changed:
The Gaddi is upright
The Tibetan, honest
But everything has changed
Each has lost his homeland
So if you give refuge
                    you invite a stranger into your home
And if you seek freedom
                    in exile you become a beggar

The world is a mandala:
red, white, green, yellow, blue
HRI, TAT, SAT, OM
OM MANI PADME HUM
Painted on sand in coloured sands
Blown away by the winds like sands
Everything is change
And the Buddha became an exile
                    In Sarnath and Bodh Gaya
where they murder for a rupee
But he lives in Thailand, Taiwan, Japan
and is re-awakening in Laos, Vietnam
from under the jackboots of the commissar:
I forgive you heel
                    for kicking me into the dust

Mother was divorced
Father is dead
Last summer's swans have flown
and left no address
The Dalai Lama says:
I bless and bless
The bored monk knows each stone
                    on the temple path
His mind is emptiness
His hands full with conch, *vajra,* bell
Gong, horn, drum
Poverty and prayer and temple service:
Life as myth and ritual

Hands are not for toil
but soft petals for ritual gesture
Eyes are not to see the slender girl
but to turn inwards
The ear in a foetus
            coiled in upon itself
yet to birth after hearing the Word

It has rained
It is yet to rain again
The temple tank has been ruffled
                    With night-storms in waves

The temple flag moves:
Is it the air that moves
Or the flag that moves?
It is the Mind that is moving.

The lotus blooms again
The lotus is yet to bloom again
                         and again
                         my illusion
My lotus-poem
I clasp you to my heart:
Father, mother, lover, teacher, god!

'For Makrand'

1

It is afternoon
In a dry season
The trellis walls of stone
Make labyrinths
Snails under foot
Moths above
Someone walks beneath the trellis
Head bowed

        Mockery from men and women in the sun

Which way is his beard pointed
Which way will madness come?
Will it rain tonight?
Will the wife return or send him to the launderers?
Let there be laundry if there is sun
Ink flows like a river
Life unravels like a poem
Lines on our hands run like rivers
Rivers get lost like lines in our poems . . .
This morning the lark rose early
Then all the crows cawed
      to announce an Indian city

When they fell on their garbage heaps
the fat bulbuls rose to the topmost tree
Puffed out against winter wind in the sun
Pecking at the berries
They ate their full
and fell to copulating in thankfulness
Four bedroomed bungalows full of servants
                    and no mistress
find no forgiveness
Where did the Ganga lose her way?
Will the Doms descend from their high homes
                    for one more body to burn?
—The world is so full of death and winter
But the bulbul sings only spring
Innocent fool! Full of cleverness
and no knowledge of evil
Whose home will you burn next
                    with your beautiful snares?
The old wives are in photographs as brides
Their hands hennaed
They know to grasp and clasp
                    but not to forego
That is not the householder's art
It is for the campy mendicant

to plow the river's flow
To know the bulbul refrain from treetop
To say who will live
                    who perish?
What will become of our 5-year-old son?
                    What of children yet unborn?
                    Are we here to mourn?
Let us build a new home
                    Order new furniture
                    Scout the Matrimonials anew
                    All is askew in a world
                    Where Queen Bee needs drones
In the world of labyrinths
There will always be walls of stone
Dry twig snails underfoot   Moths above
One autumn morning
In the heat all the pupas hatched
It rained butterflies on the world
                    a full five hours
Let it rain tears
          Let it rain poems
If you try to measure Ganga's girth
                    The string breaks
There always will be too much water in this world . . .

2

Sita sat in Asoka Vana
Awaiting Ravana
She had hacked into his computer
She knew his life-plans
Now it is War

She took her Toyota-made Pushpak
And flew to her divorce lawyer
And her grandmother
In that order
She had life plans
Peace will be made

With the sacrifice
The Ashvamedha horse will roam free
Love and Kush be there to catch it
To tell their father Rama who's what
                              and who's who
Sita will not play with fire
Son will not know his sire
Ramayanas will go on.

Ghalib Canto

'Imitation is the sincerest form of flattery'
—Wilde

Here, in a season of thorns
  a season of storms
  a season of gibbets
I remember you, Ghalib
I see you swinging from the gibbet
(though flattery saved you)
Your home now, a coal-depot
(they blackened their own faces, not yours)
I see you digging up a fresh grave
They have buried music deep, so deep

  It'll never resurrect
Give up, Ghalib!
    I WILL SING FOR YOU
    (and my friend Meena
    maddened like you
    sees your wrists sprouting leaves)
     —of song? . . .

My mother planted a garden
If I dig at Ballimaran
I'll come out at the island of Bombay
If I dig in Bombay I'll come out at Manhattan
One Walt Whitman sang there about your
                              time, Ghalib

Then Lorca and Meena
                and me
What is my mother doing in this fantasy?
                —and Meena's
Since the British came the mosque became
                              Church
Since Meena's Aramaic grandpa died
                the Church became your tavern
                (a nun recently made it a brothel)

And since mother died
                I became homeless
                Like Meena
But she found a nest in your poem
                        And in Lorca's
                And I found a nest in her
'Seeing Majnun in the desert
                my home I remembered

Lifting stone, Majnun, his head he remembered . . .'
Meena sees garden pebbles as mad whirling constellations
In my pocket I carry a little dust
                    (from Pali Hill)
          and a pocket Ghalib . . .

                              (For Meena Alexander)

Bathers at River Bhagsu Nag, Dharamsala

Wend your way
up a snaking path
To come to Bhagsu Nag:
Bhagsu came here
In search of water
And put an entire river
in his pot
The Snake-king, Nag
Uncoiled these labours
For the river was *his* habitat
Largeness of heart
Saved the day
Bhagsu became king
of hill and plain
Where the river wends it way . . .

Today the boys
are at their Sunday bath
I watch them strip to the waist
And plunge heedless, headfirst
into the pond, newly born
Their wet limbs ripple
in the morning sun
As their loincloths fall
in coils to the floor

Beads of water fall like rainbows on stone
And the snake in paradise
is aroused once more: Jai Shankar!
Jai Jai Bhole Nath!
Generosity with the young alone
Saves the old
The sun sleeps in shadows
on the bank of fallen leaves
The King, Bhagsu was young
The Snake, old
Such is the hold of old tales
Upon our young
Father and son coupled in story
and history
And water washes away everything
to a steep fall into a valley
There to snake to what sea
Which is but a vast store of actions
And re-actions . . .
You can trace your way
from the valley
up the river
to a green spring:
From that clean source
Sprang our actions and our poems
Which are told like the telling of beads
And our life was muddied

by our very hands . . .
But if all is *maya*
Then what is this body
of my lovers
rippling in the sun
Writing their reality
on the water
and the waves
Beckoning me, an old poet,
                to come . . .

Himachal Pradesh
Summer 1998

Mother

Yesterday morning
In my mid-day nap
I dreamt father clinging to me
Rather I to him: Like a plant from earth draws sap
Something was missing
Or rather, someone
It was Mother
The third, a woman, which makes two men complete
In Rodin's The Kiss it's man and woman
Intertwined like two trees
Seemingly bearing one fruit from one mouth
Or rather two girls
Supple at waist sprouting into two
from waist down
But you can trace two lineages
in that one mouth
Father and Mother to me
I am the Third
I took birth
When two women fought over a third
A Man
Young then: Atlanta's race was run
She cheated a little
Hera was displeased

Two women fought too over my birth
I am the one within whom my own seed sleeps
Through deaths and births: Nothing is lost
Nothing ever lost from the heart of a flower
                                    Or, of a girl
So through Mother's death
In my dream father and son
Cleave each to each through death and old age
An old man in dirtied clothes
While Mother died young: still a young girl
With hair spread down the back
like dark rivulets or snakes running to ground

Going room to room carrying a lamp with lightning flashes
I turn around and you're gone
Both my parents
Past and present
Old Man and boy
aged crone and girl
I have to live through many men and poems

Dead Mother return to me
Tell me, if you know, something I must learn

(After Buddhadeva Bose)

Poem for My Sister: The Garden Tomb

It is the season of gently falling rain
Autumn in other countries, here eternal summer
At the end of a long avenue of trees I have come
to look behind me and see you standing at its head
(You were always ahead of me)
And now I've stayed behind
to see you go ahead of me again
It is I who should have died
Turned that zig-zag road
to the house on the hill
of our father the owner and tenant
of our hearts
god-like, now gone
And memory settles soft as a feather
of time on my hands
when adolescence leaps out from behind
a tree/Laughs a girl's laugh
And is gone
Stay with me
Our bodies are gardens we grow
For others' use
And I do not wish to tend a grave
the rest of my days

But we are born in two times:
Our own and Eternity
And it is there the cloth is woven
for a cradle and a shroud
Here, the leaves fall
and grow into a Book
It is here we call on our ancestral home
and lay claim to the little earth
which is our own/To find it the house of the Friend
I have seen the graves of poets
In Shiraz and at home
And the script on the page
is the same script on their tombs
Birds flutter out of dovecotes at dawn

At night they turn home
But here everything is in time and out of time
Enrich me with the harvest of our day
I hear a call, 'Come'
I look for my shoes, but you go, born ahead of your time
Leaving me here, the one born after my time
See, the tree you planted sprouts green leaves
Seeing you beneath it I weep
And to see me weep you smile.

To Ghanshyam, Teacher

—And I see your sobbing face
What was it you were sobbing out?
The insults your race felt as they dragged
Cow carcasses to cobblers
to be made into shoes for well-shod feet . . .
Carcass-dragger Corpse-handler
Were they men or corpses who mouthed this?

Then out of the valley
Came a trough
Out of the trough, a plateau
Beyond the plateau a peak
And behind it the light . . .
Who lifts the mountain on a fingertip
And among the stars hangs an A

Have you counted the constellations
                    on a starry night?
Seen Siva's locks streaming on the Milky Way?
If there is god, then what about chance?
Everything is chance—
—But the Friend bestows upon a friend
                    a complete world

I thought to be Maestro
to make invisible music
But I wielded a novice's club
Breaking the easles and the jade

And I see your face
Your radiant face
Each thing remains:
Book, chair, window, lamp
Each thing hand-made, for nothing is free
Why throw this all away?

Even your ancestors had dignity:
Valmiki caught the kichaka bird
Its mate became Lament
Out of that lament came the Epic
Viraha and Karuna
Exile and Pity

Your ancestor may not have had honour
But he had dignity
And his things: net, arrow, bird-lime, basket
Rope-tether, awl, hammer, nail, sandal
We are but beasts walking on twos
Our palms turned up to the stars

When temples and pyramids
Kept time of Time
Now such temples have to be built
in our hearts

> let such a person go out to his daily work, where
> greatness is lying in ambush and some day at some turn
> will leap upon him and force him to fight for his life.

(After Rilke)

Poem: Sunday, 13 May 2007, NM

1

My sister has come to New Mexico's clear air
After a lifetime breathing Chicago petrol fumes
She has a prefab trailer home:
Adobes won't do/They block out view
She'd rather breathe in formaldehyde
See the shimmering Sangre de Cristos
Centred like some Mt Meru
She's on oxygen
(She who was my heart-lung machine)
All trussed up with tubes
that entangle our legs
as she goes about her business
Giving up a lifetime of files she's kept on me
Cooking daily as she's done for a lifetime of men
Believing still in the civilizing West
While I did my best to cosy up to de Sade
        —disillusioned with the Enlightenment . . .
     We're living at the wrong altitude
     I get altitude sickness
     I sleep a lot
     I pad around an unfamiliar house
     On sea-legs: I've not found my land-legs yet
     Just off the boat for the umpteenth time

2

The doctor will see what's wrong with me
Sister's got lots of money
She still believes in Progress
Between violent bouts of coughing
The doctors helped her lick TB twice
Now she's got something she can't lick
But my knee needs key-hole surgery
I settle for cortisone
The surgeon and I
if not blood-brothers
are brothers beneath the bone

3

Out into the sunlight
dappled by rain-clouds
The rain raining on distant peaks
Coming down in shafts
like god's mercy

4

Back home there's a double emergency
Sister's cough/my bad knee
I've to run to her aid to double-time
When alarm bells shatter
My American toilet reverie . . .

5

Nothing ever ends
It's simply our bodies giving up:
Eyelashes whiten, lungs puncture, knees buckle under
Records kept of everything:
Journeys, betrayal, love, whoring, baptisms
Women are the keepers of the tribe's myths
—My elder sister makes everything over to me
I give them over to a student-son
before I die
'Now go over back to the beginning'
a voice intones before I die, at our ending

6

We burrow into time's tunnel
Some can barely walk
Some are short of breath
But out into the open we are cast
We contemplate a wide open space
An objectless view
Which is what is finally poetry's real business.

Karmapa Journeys South

The wild geese flying south
The gooseberry frosted on the bough
The lake frozen in the valley
The grass turning dry at its edge
The Karmapa journeying south
In search of a lute and a hat

The guards let him go
The mother averted her eye
The brother did not know
The sister of 24 wished to go
With her brother in search of a lute and a hat

The wheels crushed the snow
The horses were willing to rear up
But the riders let them go free
The Karmapa had ridden a bestiary
Of wolves and goats in valleys
His stone a high throne
His toy a lamaserie made of small stones
His face shone and shone
In twenty days he came home

The High Lama broke his reverie
Twice to see this bright boy
The klieg lights blew up in his face
His face shone and his eye was clear
He ate light, slept well
And went in search of a hat and a lute

Then as if in a dream
There was no throne
There was no lamaserie
There was no lute or hat
There was none of all that

The water unfroze in the lake
The grass returned, green
Where there was a valley
There's now only a stone
And a tear unlocked in the boy's eye

He saw what the Buddha had seen
He spoke once only Tibetan
But now he does not need to use even that
                      All the world watches stunned
                      The Lama is silent
                      Like an unstrung lute
                          an empty hat

Dionysius' Basin at Nysa
(Modern Kermanshahr, Iran)

1

The infant god
must've been born bearded
like the Eastern grain
from which he springs
again and again

2

They must've bathed
The young god in this basin
Born as he was from the swamps
(He must've needed quite a bit of cleaning)
And he must've dirtied himself again
in laughter and in horseplay

3

One day the play must've turned serious
He must've learnt you can't play around
with blood, tears, semen
By that time it would've been too late
　　　to change
Tragedy was birthed for the East
As his half-brother Apollo ruled the West

4

I

Theirs was a struggle unto death
of the lion and the gryphon
of Persia/Babylon and Greece
of Winter with Spring
On the grassy uplands
The struggle goes on
Devotees bathe themselves in this basin
The King of Kings honoured him

II

This morning I stepped out of the bath basin
The mirror showed me fat and bearded
and greying
I'm descended from the King of Anshan
I mirror him
He stares out at me from the American
                    bathroom mirror
With such sad eyes.

Poem

Last night
the rain seeped into my sleep
I couldn't sleep
thinking of the Gujarati letter 'क'

My life empty as the line
that loops into a circle
only to end in an arc
like the line in the letter
Empty like an abyss in space
Like some raindrop fallen to earth.

'Lasheen'-1

1

The young Christ
has entered the Temple
He has overturned the tables
of the money-changers

He follows the footsteps
of one who changed a staff
into a serpent

The age of literacy is over
The age of miracles has begun again.

2

16-10-1970
The child born
under the harvest moon of October
It was already 5:25
and night beginning
The mother lay on the floor
and rolled over
This bonny baby with a shock of hair
stepped out into the world
and laughed

It was the beginning of a long air

3

There is no such thing
as perfect silence
Give me silence
and I shall set to music
all I hear.

4

In his palm
The forking serpent of the heart
The will to live separate
The lines to the moon
The line plunging down to life
The support systems that make a single life possible
—Will my love die before me?

5

I have entered his mind:
It is filled with liquor fumes
In his head grass grows
burns and fills a room
The smoke is heady
and goes down to a heart
A hand raises a glass
and the fire glows with its ruby-heart

6

Mr Anais Nin!
Please record how
Henry's bike veered past
The husband's car
        —whistling!

Please record how
Anais, fresh from orgasm
rose on the half-shell
of the typewriter cover
and said:
I shall pay back
        I shall record.

7

In the desert
life is air-conditioned
Insurance is sold
against the simoon
The camel is a mirage
And the caravan passes
There is no water to reflect a moon
—I bring a palmful of water
                to bring home the moon.

8

When a friend
cuts through the peninsula
I seek him out through crowds
Gifting him chicken, beer and bread.

9

At the farmhouse
young trees:
palm trees, fruit trees
I'm the young master
I may not drink or womanize
The old servants respect me
They wish all the trees to bear fruit for me.

10

I painted my vehicle
jet black
I streak in the sun
berry-brown
I shall carry you to night
and beyond
And there life will bear fruit
as only it can.
I, the child, am only its vehicle.

In Memoriam

For My Father (1917–96)

1

Flesh
Shadows
Blood
Water
My body is a shadow
haunted by water
I live in a house
made of walls of water
The monsoon washes away the ire
of my fathers from Transoxiana
A trait I share with my lover
who has become my father

2

I took my lover's hand
at Fort
showing him my childhood haunts
I caught a hand
in a city of 14 million people
and cried Father!
And you? he said

He could not see
(Busy setting his great house in order)
He passed me by in a crowd
In a city of 14 million souls
My search ended
in rage

Two days later he died of old age

3

Now my heart is a house
built of water
Shadows of a large bird fall
over a well
The bones are picked clean

All rage ends

4

And when he saw me
as one looks long
into the face of an ill-
                    beloved son
just before death
I smiled the smile of my mother
with her eyes

Our mother is Death

5

Now I talk easy with the dead
in the house of dreams
as I never did in life
The telephone is dead
Father visits my house he's built
The one with bricks of fire
And it becomes a pyramid
I carry a canoe
into dry streets
We are pharaohs in a necropolis
I awake rejuvenated

6

I have washed my hands
of my own blood
My father's house
with mirrors by the sea
moulders in a bank vault
My father has left no legacy
The leaves fall
and grow into poetry

7

We have to make threes:
In *his* dreams
my father, he and I
bicycle to his childhood home
The streets like dreams are free

8

Now blocking the gate of history
is the justice of Naushirwan
And the ghost of Ardeshir
The script on the coins is dead
My lover and I join hands in the dust
And come up with father's earth

9

My earth is an earth I made
with one-and-a-half syllables
I bypassed blood
Tears don't stain like rain
My house is a flood of poems
The dead receive no mail.

13 September 1996

Death of a Poet: 1-1-2002

1

My glasses cracked in two this morning
I obviously needed a new vision

2

On my way to the optician
I saw a Kashmiri shawl-vendor
Trying the gate of a great house
I remembered Shahid Ali

3

I want to be a golden paisley
On the black shawl of Kashmir

4

Wandering in the desert, Majnun
His home he remembered
Lifting stone, Majnun
His head he remembered

5

I want my body to be a green paisley again bent
In bed for the Great Lover

6

The desert is first made brown
So that it can later green
                              Hence green is holy
We are green first
                    And then we're dry

7

Mountains of ice   Ice like glass   We can see through them
at Kailash in Kashmir at Parnassus and Mt Meru
Faiz translating his Urdu in Beirut for transparency!
Shahid Ali dreaming snow in Arizona
                              And finding it!

8

Before this war I dreamt
it rained blood all over Mecca
Before this year ended
A friend dreamt I preached in green
                              at a dargah

9

Brown green red rain
Red rain greens then browns again
Last year's Adonis of the marble body
Is now a ruin/When I write I walk on clouds
                    Then gravity pulls me down

10

I do not want immortality in words
I just want to be immortal in life
                    sd/- Shahid Ali
Mad continuity! I drink from your glass ruby-red

11

The Phoenix burns bright on his tree
The Pole Star has fallen tonight on my house
                              my poem shall burn
Shall burn like Kashmir
Then fire shall congeal as at the first Creation
And in a bed a river sprout

A Parsee Yogi of Secunderabad, ca 1890

Muncherjee the Parsee
Sits under a tree
planted by granny
To become a yogi

(He's caught eternal
 In a zinc plate by Raja Deen Dayal)

Muncherjee doffed his topee
To grow a Hindu pigtail
And sat and sat
On a bed of nails

He occasionally ordered a khichree
And felt mystic heat
from the tiger skin
Under his seat

'O Muncherjee give up this Yogi
And return to us Parsees
Why do you your arms so flail
And sit and sit on a bed of nails?

'I wish to be One with my Maker
And do not mind being a fakir
Do not mind me turning tail
O Parsees leave me my bed of nails!

'And when upon a nail I poise
To make the Kundalini rise
I feel such bliss in my head
Better than a wank in bed.'

So Muncherjee's eyes grew wild
And from him escaped a few sighs
Could it be some holy breath
Vouchsafed to one before his death?

And then into Nirvana sail?
And under your arm your bed of nails!
Or when upon His bed you sail
Who but He can turn your tale?

(This be nectar and honey
Helped along with Parsi money)

Muncherjee Yogi sits under a tree
Planted by granny/Caught eternally
By spiritual blackmail/Impaled upon his bed of nails

Stefano Re-members the Night of Pasolini's Death, 1973

> 'To have lived, to have loved
> is the only thing that matters
> But not to have loved, not lived . . .'
> —Pasolini

That night they huddled around
Marconi's radio which crackled
like staccato gunfire, spewed out the news
like from the mouth of an idiot messenger
in a Roman play: PASOLINI MURDERED BY A BOY . . .

The father, in the city
A peasant, with the peasants' dream still
               heavy on his shoulders
     The son, still a boy . . .
—And a boy had killed a man
               And this but be a grave wrong

The dream had been killed
On the peasant father's shoulders
And now they fired from behind the father
At the son   Stefano, still a boy
Not well read in life
Going towards a city all light

Lit up as at Cinecitta Studios . . .

       . . . The dream betrayed in the peasant's
                  young shoulders

He will fill his strong farm-boy body
With spirit, with wine
Catullus will spout from his mouth
Girls sport in his bed:
All this is yet to come . . .

America shall invade the home
As they have the country
      Giving you a loaf of bread
      will steal your soul

      So that Stefano one day shall bleed
                  on the highway
      Before he becomes whole . . .

Why does everyone appear
           like everyone else
So that if Christ were to come
           to walk among us
We'd give him a stone . . .

Now Stefano is a father
And I lean on his shoulder
    And love Pasolini
And he tells me everything
    As only he can
    And I listen . . .

But the children
    his children
    Are impatient to go to the city
    Either to die at the city gate like Pasolini
        Exactly a future he predicted for them
    Or, against some new Pasolini to lift the first stone

Poem

(Navajo)

Children they say are either turquoise or silver
The boys turquoise, the rest silver
Between turquoise and silver is the bachelor
Between conquistador and the Ancient Spirit is the Indian
Mother Mary forgive us our sins
Mother Mary forgive us our sacrifice
The ground is prepared   The pilgrimage has started
The leader takes a head count
for the ascent to the Virgin of the Lakes
On the way down there will be one man less
He will lie under the ice
under the stones under a cross
There will be more springs the next thaw.

Love Poem

1

It is not man
writes language
It is language writes the man

2

I need a wall
and I create
    —on the rebound

3

Infinity has no centre
The self is centre
    but the other is infinite

4

The moment the gopi thought:
Krishna dances with me alone
Krishna fled

5

Love is
        the dance
                in Infinity

6

Mohammed said:
        Die before you die

7

A child loved me
in the present
without memory
        and without hope

8

This poem is the man written in that child's language.

(For Srinu)

6 August 2007
(Remembering Hiroshima during the Iraq War)

'I' is un-important
All I is drained out of me
It has gone into You
You are pouring into Me
I and You become indistinct: WHERE IS I
If You are Me
————

Hiroshima was not necessary to conquer Japan
Nagasaki was not necessary to end the war
————

When they tested the Bomb at Los Alamos
                    Where my sister lives
The radiation burnt everything
Leaving charred reflections of windows on walls
Like charred reflections of love on our hearts' walls
                    Now my sister is dying
                    I write this poem
Hiroshima's last survivor remembers it all   Still
————

The cloth is torn
Come love, bring me a needle
The needle of love
For the torn cloth of friendship, my friend, my love
                    Let us make love one last time . . .

My sister, my spouse lies dying
My love stitches a shroud
Death's golden needle points to the grave
I go around a graveyard but can't find your tomb

This page is a rose garden I go around
My dead blossom here
And darken my eye
            with the light of a 1,000 1,000 suns

                    (For Adnan)

Daddy

It's 11 years
Since father died
Sometimes he comes in dreams
So sorry   Like he never was in life
Once alone he screamed like he always did
                        And never, never reappeared
My sister sees him locked up in hell
I smell his approach
I feel his coat
English wool wet in the Bombay rain!
A lion in a lamb's pelt
Daddy whose bullion flashed blindly in bank vaults
And was stolen by Parsee crows within minutes of his
death
Just as his flaccid white body must've been by vultures
                                on Malabar Hill
Daddy who toiled all his life to come to this
Who forgot to make an heir for his all
'He did not love me' he complained of me
Who by then had a heart grown cold
Why then does his woollen coat smell so warm
                        in this dream-poem?

Winter Poem

(To my student, Srinath)

In dreams
           sometimes
I sleep with a boy

In dreams
           sometimes
He changes to Woman

In my dream Death thrashes his thighs

Afraid to live
I wrote love letters to life
Life did not reply

Afraid to die
I wrote love letters to death
Death did not reply

One day one winter's day
My corpse will hang   Against a purple sky

In my death life thrashes her thighs

Two Sea Poems

1. *Tsunami Sutra*

Why is the sea ebbing so far
Into itself? To crash better onto the land

Animals have inner hearing. Birds inner sight
Even reptiles sense all with their skin

Then why does the human mind set store by things
Not sense the sea of pain receding and churning
onto the shores of this world and the next?

A butterfly's wings in Chile set up a typhoon in China
I was Chuang Tzu: I slept and dreamt I was a worm

I woke up to become not poet, not worm
But a butterfly who set up a typhoon in China.

2. *Sea Sonnet*

As a child I saw three veiled ladies on the sea
Drink coconut water from shells like cracked skulls

Then I learnt Kali drank human blood thus

As an adolescent from my father's Bombay veranda
I wished upon a star and dreamt of Arabia

As a young man I got all the riches of Arabia

Then the recourso began: the stranger sea music
Lorca seafaring from Spain to New York

Columbus the Genoese humanizing the Natives
This they called the burden of the Cross:
So many lesser gods sank under the waves

Christ's tears too are salt as he trips lightly over the waters.

Jew

Brother and sister
standing at the gate
Sheep go to slaughter
Brother and sister
are learning their numbers

How many sheep
went to slaughter
Asks Mother
at the end of the day

Mother and father
exiled from the city
to the suburbs
by an irate god

Adam and Eve
having lost Paradise
learnt to delve

Paradise could be Vilna
It could be Prague or Berlin
It could be New York or Jerusalem
It could be Bombay or Turin

There is no city
Only suburb
There is no life
Only exile

Don't say I'm a singer
or a healer
A shaman or a fakir
Say I'm Adam

I lost Heaven
I found love
of man or woman
god or beast

Yet exile is not for once
But a pattern
Ask the mad prophet
He found the fall in earth's gravity

The cause of pain is separation
Life's work to heal separation
Said the teacher

I do not recognize this word
Said Mother
No language knows it
Nor any woman or man

But again Ruth stands
amid the alien corn
Again Hagar is exiled
to the desert sand

Again and again
Is an Ishmael born
With a bowl of potage
as his legacy

I sing of the earth
And the fall to the earth
I sing of the city suburb
I sing of everything I know

I know:
Every poet is a Jew

(For Wendy Steiner)

Memories of Bellagio

I sit on a rounded stone on the pier
I hear the bells toll
The wind blow
The littlest pine-needle stir   All in unison
Who stirs the wind, the pine, the bell in unison?
I breathe in and out: one with the pine, the bell, the wind
Remember Lake Galilee/Where those who believed in the
                                        body drowned!

Remember the fish and fisher on the lake
Hauling in a shoal of stars from lake bottom
Onto the land with the fish breathing for their lives
And now the stars are drowned in the lake
Just as they freely walk the clouds overhead
I have descended to the town
And with the fish-catch I count my breaths:
Inspiration/exhalation; systole/diastole
The beats of my heart
Who am I? An old man on a lake
with a promontory behind him still to climb
I begin climbing: The bell, the wind, the pine-needle
                keep me company

I am the gasping fish; I am the low glow of the fire-worm
I am alive; I did not come here to die;
I halt for breath, for pause, for thought
Who am I? Before this lake
A shade, a shadow of a shade
A ripple on the water
A cloud upon a river
My own breath upon a mirror
Who will the boatman take?
I hear the cry of the mockingbird
I begin to climb the promontory

Zib-al-Abd

1

Nigger dick
Nigger dick
Flower of hell
With a sick-sweet smell like sex
I brought it home in armfuls
to my dinner table
(The Arabs laughed)
By midnight I had to open the door to
                              let out the smell

2

Poets talk of this flower
Williams calls it the Asphodel:
Of Asphodel that greeny flower
                I come my love to speak to you
He claimed to go even to hell to find it
And having found it he found a moment's truth
        Until hell and war returned again
        And truth had to be won all over again

3

It grows abundantly on the hillsides of Palestine
And like truth it is a despised flower
No one in his right mind brings home hell
No one in his right mind loses home for hell
But having lost home men are prepared to go to hell
                              to find it again
What some call home others call truth or love or freedom

4

Bayyati the Iraqi poet lost home at twenty
He was nowhere at home for the next forty years
He was his country's slave, the slave to truth
                he searched in seven lands
In his seventieth year he was ready to die
Everything he had done was about to be undone
The children sang his songs in the streets
                in the soldiers' faces
It is as if he had brought home to them
                Armfuls and armfuls of the flower of hell
His deed done.

Sind

'I have sinned'

—Napier

It was with a Sindhi boy I first found love
He felt love but being a boy he took me from behind
Like the Holy Spirit took St. John one night on the steep
   stairway to god

It was a cold night
The train was tearing through the heart of Hindustan
And when it halted at a station
It was dawn and our love was known . . .

When the Indus meets the sea
It forgets it was the cold daughter of the snow
It becomes warm and shallow, lost in the sand
This land of sand
They call Sind

And the Arabs came
And finding Hindus there
They called this land of quicksands, Hindustan

The boys turned Turk soon enough
Eyes became mirrors for reflected lights of other gods
Warm love was pressed like wine between students and
   Master

People forgot their own names
They remembered the Name
Which too they soon forgot: Why do you ask the Name?
They asked
And remembered only love

A cowherd played the pipe
A king followed him into the forest
A son of the Mughal on his way to conquer Kabul
Remembered to note the Hindu gods in Persian

And when times turned savage opium helped the heirs to
die painlessly
And Death turned a friend when a brother turned fiend
But to face death—without opium?
Or to face life—without poetry!

The river ran red that day
The women carried their breasts on a plate for the rapists
Men carried their heads in their hands for the conqueror
And poems that mention these ravages
Now gather dust at railway stations
But the milk of Sachal, the wine of Rumi
The breath of the breeze blown through a 'ney'
                                        Say: He!

As I remember him in whose hands I died:
Thought stopped then like that night train
And my heartbeat became a public event.

Shillong, 29 October 2009

At first
it creeps upon you slowly
As a cold sting in the air
Or, wafting scent of mimosa, pineapple, fern
With shut eyes you breathe in the scent
Open them on green, green vistas
                of bamboo, cobra-lily
waiting to strike out of a childhood dream
As if seen in a mirror, with backward glance
—Where have we seen this before?—
Gauguin painted such scenes
But these chaste women, thinly gauzed
From throat to calf waft on the breeze
This must be levitation
Reflected in mountain streams
Landing on rock
Sluiced through gates at high speed
to harness electricity . . .
In fading light, a green sea
Not water but paddy
and well-drained tea

We all smell of the earth,
And again Bada Pani follows up the dusk road:
Night falling
I gather in the oncoming mist . . .
Narrow mountain gorge
A turn in the road
Suddenly, god in a cloud . . .
I have been here before:
It is the road not taken

Sang-bari: A Shower of Stones

No one bothers to pelt me with stones any more
No one calls me Majnoon any more

Bring back the boys who stoned me
—They're grown into men

Bring back Majnoon!—He died with this poem.

My Great-grandfather

A Parsee hat-maker
glued paper together
into a thick board
Then he cut it shaped it curved it
in cowhoof shape (out of Hindu respect)
to fit the refugee Parsee head
Next he painted everything black
and then polished that blackness to a shine
Last he touched it up with gold points, 18 kt.
Like golden stars in a dark night.

A Sufi saw a star on his head
'You're a diamond!' he said
Great-grandfather became a jeweller
Operating out of a hole-in-the-wall in the bazaar
He gained entry to the best homes in the city
The choicest pieces he kept for his daughter (adopted).

I share a star with my great-grandfather
Cancerians both (by the moon): Our names begin with an
    'H'
How have I bridged to him
by way of repaying generational debts?
I have adopted no child
I am a refugee once again
I have gone over to the enemy in friendship
Forgive me, ancestor! I'm too modernized.

This Spring a Koel Turning in a Tree

This spring a koel turning in a tree
Black and goldbrown/red eye in a green neem tree
I did not hear I only see
In my mind's eye
Black gold and green: a koel turning in the tree

It is morning   It could be high noon
It is Spring   It could be Summer's green
And leaves falling green to brown
And black wings turning in a tree
The wind rising as at dawn

It could be night
And as at old age a man perceives his youth
I still see the morning bird upon the tree
Turning and turning upon a branch
As if bound and caged in love for a leaf
                                        a fall

Then I suddenly turned
Heard the leaf fall
Saw night descend
And remembered the scream of the koel.

Remembering My Last American Lover . . .

He wasn't American, at all:
He was Bermudan: a floating Chicagoan at the Continental
    Baths
Brown of the earth, soft earth after squall
I was quiet, subdued
He tall, all stretched out in a hired bed
Going from sleeping north-south to east-west
giving head
the longitude of America/latitude of Bermuda
lassitude of India where no longitude matters
(It's the latitude, the British would lament
too hot near the Tropics)
And he take me, take me to India
              anywhere really (an out-of-work model

Too old to be an ersatz Belafonte
In any Sears Roebuck catalogue
Spurned by every agency at 32
I've forgotten his name: let's call him John)
And I: Take me, take me
Before email, before cell phone   All of 20
set sail for the Holy Land, no less
Getting out of bed I imagined his feet pointed east
No, not really: Hamlet-like he pointed north/north-west

For Benazir

Four rivers flow within you
Five fingers caress you
Rivers of fingers run to the Sea
(sometimes a word can open a sea)
The sand angel awaits you
To enfold you in your four thousand eight hundred acres
   of land
There you'll be safe
Land-locked
As in a bank
By Death's miserly angel
Your children's fingers try
               to pry open the stone
The worm within does its ministry
The worm within did its ministry
Only your five blood-red fingers ran to the sea

                          (After Rafael Alberti)

Rickshawallah

The jazz of the city
beaten out on your tin can
by muscled arms
waxing/waning

moons of Eid
many Eids
coalesce in bed
as on a street

Such traffic of love!
—and no stop signs . . .
Pitch, tar, toss, fling
From the farthest shore

Or highest balcony
Such love as no boy can bear
Or know
—Release me!

Into the dust and chaos of the city!

Trade

('The Weaver, the Watchman, the
Rickshawallah . . .')

1

The weaver died
and left his loom
half-undone the cloth
Its warp and weft
Deft as I am
how can I touch a loom
whose cloth will unwind
for millions of words?

2

The watchman dark
still shakes his stick
at me in that memory
I wished to clasp him
He wished to book my theft
How tell my dark watchman
                    from the dark?
—I let him go

3

I wished to go wish Eid
to my Moslem friends
I could not find the fare

At my door stood
a young driver
if only he'd look:
I took him for a ride
                in my mind
Then feeling abashed I fell to prayer

Coda

I

How forget the young bridegroom
Who built me a house
                brick by brick?

If I'd loved him
his world would've crumbled
                all in a heap:
I blessed his bride's labour
And moved into an empty house
                Populated now by poems . . .

II

Of the yarn I thought to make
a textile set with sun, moon and star

But found it a text
With dashes, dots, muttered words

(After Kabir)

Mother's Absence

(For Joy Roy)

'Absence, large as Mt Lebanon'
—Adonis, Syrian poet

You move around her rooms
Feeling her air cling around you
And her absence palpable
As the three arches in the middle of the room
That being Nothing allow passage
from Something into some other thing:

Or, that space within her pitcher
Into which you pour all your substances
Or her empty space at table
Which indeed is your true sustenance
Or, still, that still flowering tree
Each Spring birthing, shrieking red
From whose arms you see her fling
Great emptiness out for you

So that if at all you move, you move
Like a bird that feels the empty air he moves through

(After Rilke)

Eurydice
(Or, the 16-Year-Old Saira Banu)

There was always within me a little girl
Who danced with my sister under the cherry
Who slept in my ear when I slept
Who leapt out of my mouth when I spoke
So that the whole world stood transfixed?

The girl walked with me the sea-city's streets
And took into herself the sea, the city, the streets
The towers and the hovels and the men inhabiting them
And when they slept they slept with me

So that if a 16-year-old nymph
Sang a love song in a movie
It was sung to me: It will be a great favour
                              if you let me love
So were many wet nights put to sleep with me

Orpheus went to Hell to bring back Eurydice
So did I when the little girl in me died
It was at the moment of looking back at her
That Eurydice was lost but Orpheus saved

A thousand things are born from Being
But Being itself is born from Non-Being.

(After Rilke)

New Year's Eve in the Gulf, 1994

Why have I come to a country not my own
and yet not another?
It is not Serendip:
There are no steles to read its history by
The sun bleaches all things

Where are the Arabs, I asked
Pearl-fishing or dhow-building
All I heard were hired hands
Even the birds of home were those of passage here:
Parrot and mynah and gull

They need no passports
Those that come and go generations
in Sindbad's dreams
they have become Suleimani from Ceyloni
that is to say, from something into nothing

Once they greedily fingered the rupiah here
What they could get of it
And lived in barsatis on the beaches
looking for dhows bringing in coir
to caulk broken beached ones
How many sails I saw drift by my boyhood window

Off to the Arabian Sea
though our world bound by a garden-wall then
had no place for Arabia:
(Only Mother, vast as Asia
and Father, remote as god)

Then life was one long Arabian Nights
I was Ali Baba and Morgiana
I was her knife and the breast that received it
I was Arab and Jew and the Magus
While boringly remaining myself

When did the X'mas card figures become real?
In that taxi to Bethlehem where the fellah
sat fingering money foisted on him by a foreign power
right in his very home

And I did not weep but said:
THESE PEOPLE'S MONEY IS NOT THEIR OWN?

Even their dreams are not their own any more
Thesiger found a lot of boys naked under their cloaks
To undulate with in the dunes
But where he did that, today is Karama Circle
And the Gulf is only another name for greed, he says

At Eton they boxed his ears for lying
about cheetah hunts (Lord Chelmsford's son)
But the Orient was oriental then
And no amount of political correctness will will it away

146

And all the world's gold was lost for a pepper corn
Pepper I'd seen glistening in rain on the Malabar ghats
What was that mad boy not doing to die driving that
   night?
Did he not know of the snail roaming worlds at home
        in its shell?
Of Sindbad blown by the Trades; returning to earth
        thrown down by rocs?

Of steles that hermetically keep secrets from
        minds while proclaiming them to sight?
Who owns what? The petrol will dry up.
Karama Circle return to desert
But the walls of Gondwana or Gaddara or Sheba
        glisten on till the end of time.

The Death Doctor

I met him on a plane
And since he was beautiful
I instantly fell in love with him
(I've forgotten his name
Though I knew the same
by peeping into his passport
as he filled in the disembarkation card)
He told me he was
                    The Death Doctor

His patients were handsome men
beautiful girls
old ugly women
sweet little children
Even Ingrid Bergman in her last illness
(Alas! Artur-Vivante had seen her in her first confinement)

Cancer can come to anybody
And it can come from almost anything
An Indian granddad on a previous plane
told me of his brilliant little grandson
who first lost a leg/then a hand
then another leg/then another hand
They brought him home The American doctors continued
 treatment FREE

—Please let him die!
At his school, for his bravery, they planted a tree
(It was the high tension wire over their $100,000 home . . .)

Death surrounds me!
These three years I rush to sister
Through the world's airports
in a wheelchair—
Take me to Chimayo, NM FAST
before my sister dies
self-scourged like the Mexican Penitentes
The martyred self of Simone Weil, the Flagellante
in her glass-bubble home
with a perfect plastic dome
Letting in a saintly light . . .

Death Doctor walks here each spring:
He's had enough of Siena's Cancer Hospital
Walking away his late spring in the Sangre de Cristos
He crushes underfoot bulbs peering out
                    like dead men's eyes

In Ambrogio Lorenzetti's *Well-governed City*:

*. . . The sense is of the artist having picked up Siena entire, and
redistributed it along the spread of a single wall over forty-foot
long. Lorenzetti gives us access, through cutaway views, windows,*

booths and loggias, to a great range of human activity; he unifies it all not through any systematic perspective but through intuitive spatial organization.'

Intuitive
Spatial
Organization
To flee space
To free space
To walk in a free place
To make a new space

'200 years later Breughel stopped in Siena on his way South, and was permanently marked by Lorenzetti's Visionary Space. Both artists share the high horizon, the visual field filled with complex incident. Both invite the spectator to respond to a sequence of pictures-within-the-pictures; to walk a road, to make an itinerary. Their pictures create, in a manner marvellously akin to cinema, the narrative of the eye's wandering in the crowded world.'

To walk a road
To make an itinerary
Wandering in the crowded world
(Lorenzetti's)
And Whitman's wide open spaces:
The open road leads to the used-car lot

The Mortuary is fled by taking the Open Road
The, there be
The Ill-governed City
City of Plague
Sex and Death
There will always be girls
There will always be Mother
                    to do the laundry
                    fix the Sunday pasta
God is for three occasions:
Birth-marriage-Death
Now only, two
For who has time for the third?
Let's just be friends:
Mr Papadopoulos, the Olympia Air steward
has a firm-hand grip
A perpetual smile
And a permanent hard-on   Forget Dr Death
                    At the terminal are so many roving eyes.

At Seven Tombs, Golconda 10-10-10

> 'The stone lives, the flesh dies
> —We know nothing of Death'
>
> —William Carlos Williams

1

In a dry bed
Seven breasts
Afloat on the warm day
The cupola of the inverted sky upheld
As a falcon whirls, whirrs the dry air
              and lands on a dry twig
As a master-planner must've
              to master Death . . .

2

I bring my new love
into a stream's dry bed
And sing old songs
to stir a passion
that is not there . . .
We are both, two girls
Who must but sing Death
Since neither of us can love
              nor birth . . .

3

Where is all the water gone?
Here, there is a deep well
And they drew out water
Cool, hid between great rock clefts
deep in the earth
To wash dead bodies
still warm with life
laid to rest
In the cool, dark earth.

4

The emperor must have
laid down his lust
to rest, damp
            in the cool, dark earth

5

How many slaves and slave girls slaved
In the mortuary and the harem?
On a hot day
The hot air
stirs a vision:
I see
On a log
The rajah's seven wives

Seated serially
The youngest first
Her dark breast naked
And last
Seven paces behind her
The first
Her dugs drawn from giving
Dried of moisture as this earth
And the new wife's uplifted
as if in echo to the first's

                    yet to give fruit, in birth . . .

6

Or, is it the King's Mother I see
Maa Sa'ab: Queen Mother
          Lady Who Couldn't Capitulate
On whose dried lake-bed
They built the tawdry city
I dwell in

7

I, the blind poet Hashmi
of the harem
imitating woman-talk:
'If you come near me
I'll turn my face

And if you touch my hand
                I'll push you away . . .'
Women's talk became
                The coin-of-the-realm

8

Thus, Quli Qutub
A falcon wheeling over the dry plain
Far as the eye can see
All the way to Bijapur
From Bala Hissar, the topmost promontory
                wails in Dakhni, nights:
'I cannot drink without the Beloved
I cannot live without the Beloved'
—The Beloved being but another name for WATER

9

Fire and water:
Phallic canon-balls from great canons
                blew off the enemy
The Fort never fell
until—
Some opened the door
        from within:
A traitor with a woman's wiles
The victor but a traitor's wife . . .

Water and fire:
The King's fifty-five concubines
astride a canon
blown off by a canon
              at his merest displeasure

                    (As at the world's displeasure this Well
                            still drowns lover after lover . . .)

But mistress know
how to please
To sing, dance
recite rhymes
titillate
scintillate
Even now I hear
The tinkling bells of their feet . . .
Their tomb-cupolas
imitating their great breasts, upturned
              the earth's womb:
There being no straight lines in nature

10

Air stirs
a morning glory
swaying on its slender neck
facing Mecca to the West

It is the time of noon-prayer
Moses must've struck water from rock
                at such a time:

I hear its gush
It fills the bed
These sheets are wet . . .

Whabiz

1

Four in the afternoon sun
Still napping:
Whabiz! Wake up
You look like a Negro!
(Thus Mother ca 1963)
She ran off to America
WASP country
Married one
Taught college—Blacks
Left them half her wealth
The coroner entered her race as
                WHITE

2

A Black dance teacher
Wanted to rent
She pirouetted through sister's
      parquet floors—
—Rich!
 She worked hard, I said
And she:
 —So did we for 200 years

3

I

She could cook up feasts
In her last illness
She would dream feasts
And not eat
Dead of anorexia
Eat! The voice of the Thunder God
And smash!
The child's face would be slammed
into a plate of wasted food

Give us this day
            our daily scrap of love . . .!

II

Other siblings
gorged
couldn't get enough of the breast
Now they go through Dieting courses
Dead of overeating:
'Food, sex, money are dangerous things' (the Shastras)
At Auschwitz souls begged bodies:
Simone Weil simply offered up to them her body

4

I
My sister, my spouse:
The mosquito-net is the bridal veil
Where you dreamt romance
        from *The Mill on the Floss*
Read under a blanket
by torchlight
(Young minds would be addled by romance)

I bought you
Your first saree
Pleated it at the waist for you, too
Another gay friend's pain
        earned him a hit from mother's shoe
Dear, O dear what's a gay man to do?

How they roared at the Passport Office
To see your name entered on my passport
        against 'SPOUSE'
Now that you're dead
I could get that entry out

So they say: Till death do us part . . .

II
The resemblance
between
a violin case
and a coffin:

Tennessee loved
his sister's violinist-lover
The boy died

Every violin case
appeared in a coffin
To Tennessee's guilty eye

5

On a cold night she died
By morning she was ash
Enshrined in a vase
              on the mantelpiece

The wind carried the ash
Some settled on Kailash
Some at Pacific bottom
So much detritus in my heart

6

Finale:
Ariadne gave Theseus
the red thread of memory
to kill the Minotaur

Theseus married Ariadne
And abandoned her at Naxos
Dionysius wed her

Theseus—Minotaur—Dionysius
Theseus is our lover
The Minotaur, our father
Dionysius, death.